GREAT CIVILIZATIONS

The Incas

Longman

Contents

Top: Modern Quechua Indians, the descendants of the Incas, at a festival in Peru. Centre: Llamas on the high grasslands of the Andes mountains. Below: Peruvian boys climbing over the ruins of an Inca building. Previous page: An Inca wooden 'quero', or goblet.

Editorial

Author
Anne Millard

Series Editor
Frances M. Clapham

Editor
Elizabeth Wiltshire

Illustrator
Richard Hook

LONGMAN GROUP LIMITED
London
Associated companies, branches and representatives throughout the world

First published 1980

Designed and produced by Grisewood & Dempsey Ltd,
Grosvenor House, 141-143 Drury Lane,
London WC2
© Grisewood & Dempsey Ltd, 1980

Printed by South China Printing Co., Hong Kong

BRITISH LIBRARY CATALOGUING IN PUBLICATION DATA

Millard, Anne
The Incas.—(Great civilizations; 7).
1. Incas—Juvenile literature
I. Title II. Series
980'.004'98   F3429
ISBN 0-582-39071-0

NEAR EAST	ELSEWHERE	AD 1100
1104 Crusaders capture Acre		
	1151 End of Toltec empire in Mexico	
	1168 The Aztecs leave Chicomoztoc Valley for the Valley of Mexico	
1174 Saladin conquers Syria		
	1240 End of empire of Ghana in Africa	
1260 Mamluk Turks control Egypt and Syria		
1291 Saracens (Muslims) capture Acre from Christians	**1271** Marco Polo, the Venetian explorer, travels to Cathay (China)	
1301 Osman, founder of Ottoman Turks, defeats Byzantines	**1300** Ife kingdom in Nigeria	**1300**
	1325 Aztecs found Tenochtitlan	
	1368–1644 Ming dynasty in China	
1379 Timur the Lame (Tamerlane) invades Persia		
1390 Turks conquer Asia Minor		**1400**
1402 Timur the Lame completes conquest of most of Ottoman empire	**1421** Peking becomes capital of China	
1453 Ottoman Turks capture Constantinople (Byzantium) which becomes their capital	**1486** Bartolomeu Diaz rounds Cape of Good Hope	
	1492 Christopher Columbus discovers the New World	**1500**
1520 Suleiman the Magnificent of Turkey begins 46-year reign	**1521** Hernan Cortés conquers Tenochtitlan	
	1522 First circumnavigation of the world by Magellan's expedition	
	1530 Death of Babur, founder of Mughal dynasty in India	
	1554 Turks conquer coast of North Africa	
1571 Battle of Lepanto: combined papal and Venetian fleet defeats the Turks	**1577–1580** Francis Drake sails round the world	**1580**

The Incas

The Inca empire was built up in the 15th century and lasted less than a hundred years. It covered a vast area between the coast of the Pacific Ocean and the jungle of the Amazon Basin. Centred in the Andes mountains, it stretched from modern Colombia south through Ecuador and Peru into Chile and Argentina.

The ruling Incas were all members of one family, but they controlled some six million people. They did this by governing with ruthless efficiency and strictness. Every detail of daily life was under government control. All land belonged to the state and everybody had to do some work for the government as a kind of tax. People in need were fed and clothed. The Incas built a network of roads so that their armies and messengers could travel swiftly all through their great empire.

The Incas had many skilled craftsmen, including weavers, potters and goldsmiths. Gold was to prove their undoing, for stories of an empire rich in gold came to the Spaniards who had just conquered Mexico. In 1532 a small Spanish expedition landed on the coast of Peru to see whether these stories were true. Incredibly, they managed to capture the Inca emperor and gain control of his empire. The old ways of life disappeared under Spanish rule. There is now little to remind us of the Incas except a few examples of their pottery and metalwork and the ruins of once great cities perched high in the Andes mountains.

Above: A gold and turquoise beaker decorated with the heads of gods. It was made by the Chimu people who were conquered by the Incas. Below: Machu Picchu, an Inca stronghold built high among the peaks of the Andes mountains.

Setting the Scene

The Inca empire stretched from Ecuador to Chile, and ruled people in deserts, mountains and jungle.

Llamas on the high grasslands of the Andes mountains. The Incas used to graze their herds of llamas in these areas.

In the middle of the 15th century a vast empire grew up in South America. It stretched for some 3200 kilometres (2000 miles) along the west coast, centred on what is now Peru. The peoples who lived there were united under the rule of the Incas until, only a hundred years later, the Spaniards conquered the land and destroyed many of the old ways of life.

The land they lived in

The countryside and climate in which people live have always played an important part in deciding the kind of lives they lead and the ways in which they organize themselves. Peru, the centre of the Inca empire, is a land in which both the climate and the scenery are completely different between the coast in the west and the mountains in the east.

Near the coast of Peru is a dry, lifeless desert. In the north plants only flower for a short time after the rare but heavy rainstorms. But crossing the deserts are small rivers which flow down from the great Andes mountains through fertile valleys.

CHRONOLOGY

AD 1100 The Inca family under their leader Manco Capac settle in the highland town of Cuzco

1300 Inca Roca becomes the first leader to take the title Sapa Inca

1438–1493 Inca empire established in Peru and the neighbouring areas by Pachacuti Inca Yupanqui (1438–1471) and his son Topa Inca Yupanqui (1471–1493)

1493–1525 The reign of Huayna Capac, who conquers the kingdom of Quito

1525 Huascar (1525–1532) becomes Sapa Inca

1532 Atahuallpa (1532–1533) defeats his brother Huascar in civil war, but is later captured by the Spaniards

1533 Atahuallpa is executed by the Spaniards. Pizarro and his men conquer the Incas and rule the country as a Spanish province

1572 Defeat and capture of Tupac Amaru, the last Inca ruler

8

Along the coast a belt of cold sea water, the Humboldt Current, sweeps up from the south. These cool waters are alive with fish which provide food for the local people.

Behind the narrow coastal strip rise the towering Andes mountains. Many of their peaks are covered with snow all year long. It is too high and too cold for men to live there. Between the mountains, however, are grass-covered grazing lands, and fertile well-watered valleys. This was the heart of the Inca empire. Farther east the land drops steeply into the great basin of the river Amazon. Here the rainfall is heavy and lush tropical plants grow in the hot climate. The Incas never went far into this dense jungle.

Lakes have formed in some of the valleys between the mountains. The most famous of these is Lake Titicaca. It lies 3812 metres (12,506 feet) above sea level. A legend tells how the Sun God created Manco Capac and his sister on an island in this lake. From them, it was said, were descended all the later Inca emperors.

Who were the Incas?

The name 'Inca' was originally given to people who belonged to a group of families from Cuzco, which is high up

The extent of the Inca empire by AD 1530. It stretched for some 3200 kilometres (2000 miles) from north to south along the west coast of South America. An efficient system of roads linked the capital, Cuzco, with all the regions of the empire. The Incas called their country 'Tahuantinsuyu', the land of the Four Quarters.

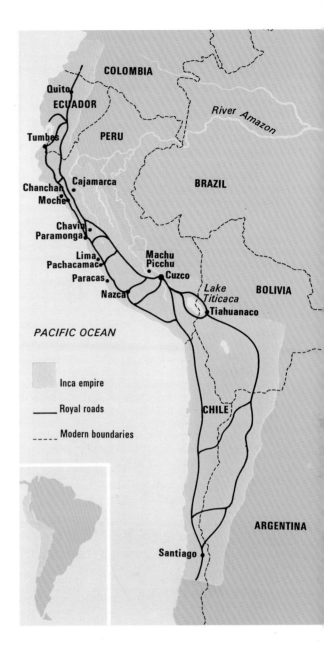

The lush, tropical rain forest of the Amazon Basin which lay to the east of the Inca empire. It was a source of fruit and exotic feathers much prized by the Incas.

in the mountains. These families were all related, and from them came the leaders who won the empire. Later a special decree gave the name Inca to everyone who spoke the same language as the first families. A modern version of this language is still spoken. It is called Quechua.

When the Spaniards arrived they used the name Inca for all the people who lived in the empire, whatever language they spoke. The Spaniards spoke of the ruler of the empire as *The Inca*. Even today it is often not clear what people mean by the name. In this book we call the ruler the emperor, and all the people he ruled over the Incas.

Hunters and farmers

The Inca families of Cuzco did not begin to conquer their vast empire until the reign of the great Pachacuti Inca Yupanqui (AD1438–1471), but the history of the people of Peru goes back a long, long way before that. The first people in the area were hunters, who also collected plants that were good to eat. Then some of them learned how to sow seeds, and settled down in one place while their crops grew. They also learned how to tame and use the local animals. They had changed from hunters to farmers. Other people settled on the coast, where large fishing villages grew up and prospered.

We know about these people only from the things they made and left behind them, for no one in South America could write before the Spaniards came. The people who lived along the coast were very skilled potters long before Inca times. These early people were also clever weavers, and some of their cloth, buried in the dry sand, has lasted until today.

Not long before the Inca times a great empire grew up along the coast of Peru. It was ruled by the Chimú people. They were skilled builders and farmers,

A bowl made in the form of an animal. It belongs to the Chavín period, long before the Incas. It was made in about 700 BC and probably represents a puma or jaguar, both members of the cat family. They are shown on many Peruvian objects and seem to have played an important part in religion from earliest times.

Pottery vessels in the form of human figures like these can tell us much about the way people looked and dressed. The figure on the right is a warrior. These pots were made by the people of the Mochica civilization of Peru between 100 BC and AD 600.

potters and metalworkers. The Incas learned a great deal from them.

Learning about the Incas

The Spaniards arrived in Peru in the early 16th century and soon gained control of the Inca empire. They began to take an interest in the history and customs of their new subjects and wrote down fascinating accounts of them. Much of our knowledge of the Incas comes from their books. The Incas themselves had no system of writing. Instead stories of the past had been handed down from one generation to the next. Information passed down like this often gets changed in the telling. Even so, some scholars think that the traditional list of emperors is correct. The first Inca ruler, Manco Capac, probably lived some time in the 12th century. After him came seven rulers about whom little is known.

In 1438 the ninth ruler, Pachacuti Inca Yupanqui, came to the throne. He was a brilliant general. One by one he conquered the neighbouring tribes and brought them under Inca rule. His son Topa Inca Yupanqui was another great general. He conquered the Chimú empire on the north coast. Together, Pachacuti and Topa established the organization which ran the empire firmly and well. This was a staggering achievement in such a short time.

The next emperor, Huayna Capac, conquered new lands in the north. Much of his time, however, was spent in dealing with rebellions of tribes in

INCA DESCENDANTS

The Quechua Indians who live today in the highland region of Peru are descended from the Incas. Their hair is straight and black, and their skin is brown. These Indians seem short compared with many modern people; the average height for a man is only about 160 centimetres (5 feet 2 inches). They have powerful chests and larger lungs than most people, which help them to breathe in the thin mountain air. They can lead hard-working lives while visitors to the mountains are soon gasping.

the empire. For by now the empire was almost too large. It took too long for armies to travel from one place to another to keep everyone under control. Important decisions had to be taken by the emperor himself, and this led to delays and difficulties.

The end of the empire

After the death of Huayna Capac, his son Huascar became emperor. He was overthrown by his brother Atahuallpa

A modern Quechua Indian woman and her child. They are descended from the Incas.

in a terrible civil war which was barely over when the Spaniards arrived. The empire had been very badly weakened by this war, and it did not take the Spaniards long to gain control of it. They soon reorganized it and almost all the old customs were lost forever.

The Inca empire lasted for barely a hundred years, but it was so cleverly built up, organized and controlled that it deserves to be remembered as one of the great empires of the past.

A gold ceremonial knife, inlaid with turquoise, which was made by the Chimú people of Peru. It dates from about AD 1200 and was probably an offering to a god, perhaps the one who is represented on the handle. The Chimú were expert metalworkers and the Incas probably learnt much from them.

A BEARDED STRANGER

In about 1523 a group of Indians called the Chiriquana, who came from lands to the east of the empire, raided an Inca settlement. With them was a strange man with light-coloured skin and a beard. He was the first white man the Incas had ever seen. He was a Spaniard called Alejo García, who had been shipwrecked on the coast of Brazil, and had worked his way westwards and joined the Chiriquana Indians. He was killed on the return journey before he could write about his adventures. Soon there were more stories of white strangers in the north. These were Spaniards who were in Central America.

The Emperor and his Nobles

The Emperor was descended from the Sun. His rule was absolute, but he slept on the floor like his subjects.

The first Incas were a large family who settled in Cuzco, in the Peruvian Andes, some time in the 12th century AD. During the 15th century the Incas built up an empire which contained many different tribes. The members of the Inca family became a noble class, who lived in different parts of the empire and helped the emperor to rule it.

The Sapa Inca
The Inca, the emperor, took the title of the Sapa Inca, 'only emperor'. It was believed that he was descended from the Sun god and so was himself a god on Earth, where his word was law. As the emperor Atahuallpa told Pizarro, the Spanish conqueror: 'In my kingdom no

The Temple of the Three Windows at Machu Picchu. One of many Inca legends tells how the first ruler, Manco Capac, emerged with other members of the family from three 'windows', or openings, in a mountain to found the Inca empire.

INCA EMPERORS

This list of 13 emperors was given by the Incas to the Spaniards:

Manco Capac (who ruled some time in the 12th century AD)
Sinchi Roca
Lloque Yupanqui
Mayta Capac
Capac Yupanqui
Inca Roca
Yahuar Huacac
Viracocha Inca
Pachacuti Inca Yupanqui (1438–1471)
Topa Inca Yupanqui (1471–1493)
Huayna Capac (1493–1525)
Huascar (1525–1532)
Atahuallpa (1532–1533)

bird flies, no leaf quivers, if I do not will it.'

The emperor was so far above the ordinary people that no one, not even the daughters of neighbouring rulers, was really good enough to be his queen. It became the custom for the emperor to marry another descendent of the Sun, his own sister. She was called the *Coya*. The ruler had the right to choose his heir. Although he usually chose one of the Coya's sons, it was not necessarily the eldest, but the ablest who was chosen. Emperor Mayta Capac is said not to have chosen his eldest son as his heir because he was too ugly! The emperor did not always have his way. The nobles could object to his choice of an heir if they felt very strongly about it. Pachacuti, one of the greatest of all emperors, was not the first choice.

The emperor was allowed to choose his other wives, which we can call 'secondary wives', from the most beautiful girls in the empire. He could have several hundred secondary wives, according to some reports, and many of them had children. The emperor Topa Inca is said to have had 92 children.

A family of nobles
The emperor ruled his vast empire with the help of officials. These were all noblemen. Army officers and priests were also drawn from the noble classes. They came next in importance after the emperor. In the early days of the Inca empire they were all descendants of former emperors. The emperor Pachacuti needed more men of the highest rank to help him run the empire. He made a special law by which people who spoke the Inca language and had the same customs would now become noblemen. Many of them became officials in newly conquered territories.

Nobles had many special privileges and rewards. They could ride in litters, and their clothes and ornaments were much finer than those of the ordinary people. They were also allowed to wear large gold ear-plugs. The emperor gave them wives, servants, gold and silver

The emperor Topa Inca Yupanqui and his 'Coya' (queen) being carried in a litter by nobles. This drawing is from a book written by Poma de Ayala at the beginning of the 17th century. He was the grandson of an Inca official and was anxious to keep a record of Inca customs and ways of life before they disappeared under Spanish rule. Many of his drawings are illustrated in this book.

objects, land and llamas. They did not have to pay taxes and they were supported by the government.

A second group of nobles consisted of the *curacas*. This included the chiefs of conquered areas, who had been allowed to keep their former positions. Curacas were divided into four ranks according to how many men they were in charge of. The most important curacas had 10,000 men under them, the least important had 100. Curacas could pass their rank on to their sons.

The life of the emperor

When a new emperor began his reign there was a great public ceremony at which he put on a special fringe or headband, which was the mark of his new status. The fringe was about 10 centimetres (4 inches) wide and was decorated with gold tubes and red tassels. Into it were put two feathers from a rare bird.

The emperor's clothes and ornaments were in the same style as those of his subjects but were much richer and finer. His clothes were made specially for him by the Chosen Women (see page 18). One Spanish writer said that the emperor 'never put on the same dress twice, but gave it to one of his relations'. The emperor's gold ear-plugs were especially large and fine.

Part of a colourful feather poncho made for a nobleman. Exotic feathers were brought from the jungle and were worn only by nobility. Notice the red squares. The Incas were very fond of colourful geometric patterns like this.

The emperor's meals were served by some of his wives, using vessels of gold and silver. Everyone entering the emperor's presence had to remove their sandals. But only a few greatly favoured subjects were allowed to come near to him. Most people could only catch a glimpse of him through a screen.

The emperor visited all the parts of his empire as often as he could. When he travelled he was carried on a fine litter, and special houses were built all along the way for him to stay in. He slept on the floor, like all his people, but on a cotton quilt with coverings of the finest quality. The Spanish conquerors sent the emperor Atahuallpa's bed coverings to King Philip II of Spain, who used them on his own bed.

When the emperor died some of his wives and servants offered to follow their master into the Next World. They were strangled at a great feast after they had been made very drunk. The emperor's body was specially treated to preserve it and then it was carefully, wrapped in fine cloth. The 'mummy' (as a body preserved like this is called) was looked after and waited on, just as if it was alive. Once a year, at the great Sun festival, the mummies of all past emperors were carried in procession.

Warriors and Warfare

In the early days of their history the Incas were surrounded by rival tribes who were as strong as they were. They often had to fight hard if they were to survive.

In the reign of Pachacuti Inca Yupanqui many new lands were brought under Inca control and several tribes were defeated. The empire was extended even farther by his son Topa Inca Yupanqui, who conquered the powerful Chimú empire on the north coast.

The Inca army was successful because it was well trained, well organized and, compared with most of its enemies, well armed. When it was marching it was also well supplied with food and medicines which were kept in special storehouses along the roads. All able-bodied men probably served in the army at some time during their lives. This formed part of their *mita*, a tax which was paid by working for the emperor. In this way most men had some training in the use of weapons.

Arms and armour

The Incas knew about and used bows and arrows and spears, but these were not the main weapons of their army. At the beginning of a battle Inca warriors would open fire with slings and *bolas*, while they were still some distance from the enemy. After this first attack, the Inca warriors moved in for hand-to-hand fighting. The main weapon was a club, which was a heavy piece of wood weighted with a stone at one end. Sometimes this weight was shaped like a star with a number of copper or bronze points. The Inca sword was a heavy weapon made of hard wood. There were also battle axes which were made with stone or copper heads.

Inca warriors used thick quilted cotton tunics for armour. Sometimes they wrapped lengths of quilted material round their bodies. On their backs they wore wooden shields for extra protection. They carried small round or rectangular shields, which were sometimes painted or decorated with feathers. The warriors protected their heads with helmets made of wood or cane.

Into battle

The emperor himself often led the army into battle, but he also appointed a close relative to command it and to act for him. Generals and high-ranking army officers were noblemen. Soldiers were divided into companies, each of which bore its own standard.

Priests travelled with the army. They prayed and made sacrifices and tried to weaken the enemy by magic. Each company of soldiers usually carried a sacred object of their own to protect them and to bring them luck.

The army marched into battle to the music of trumpets, drums and flutes. Soldiers who showed special bravery in fighting were given metal objects to wear as medals. There were also other awards for bravery. Common soldiers received gifts from the emperor, such as clothing. A noble who distinguished himself was given more valuable presents, including extra wives.

When a soldier killed an enemy he often tried to keep the body. He made his victim's teeth into a necklace, the shinbones into flutes and the skull into

Pachacuti Inca Yupanqui leading his men into battle against a rival tribe. He is wearing a red cloak and feathered helmet. The Incas hurl stones at their enemy with slings. These are whirled round and round the head to gain speed before one end is let go to release a stone. One Inca brandishes a star-headed mace. 'Bolas', made of stones fastened to lengths of string, could be thrown from a distance and would wrap themselves round the enemy's arms or legs.

a drinking cup. These were highly prized and showed what a great warrior he was.

Inca rule

When the battle was over, defeated enemy leaders were executed only if they refused to accept Inca rule. Some were sacrificed. Most of the conquered people were made citizens of the empire. Many of their chiefs were allowed to keep their rank, and their sons were sent to Cuzco to be trained as good Incas. They were then allowed to return to their fathers.

Conquered peoples were expected to speak the Incas' language, worship their gods and follow their way of life. Inca officials made a thorough survey of everything in a conquered area. If the people were rebellious, they were sometimes made to live in other parts of the empire. At other times Inca settlers were brought in to show them how to do things the Inca way.

Organizing the Empire

Life for most people in the Inca empire was ruled in every way by the government.

The modern city of Cuzco high in the mountains of Peru. Cuzco was the capital of the Inca empire and the seat of government. To the right is the site of the original main square where all important ceremonies used to take place.

Inca government was well organized. Although life for most people in the empire was probably not very exciting, at least they felt safe and knew that they would not be allowed to starve. Work was divided in special ways in order to provide food for everyone. From childhood to old age, everyone knew his place in society and the work he was expected to do to make the empire run smoothly and well.

Division of land and labour
All the land in the empire was divided into three parts. Crops grown in the first part went to the gods, those in the second to the emperor, and those in the third to the peasants. The peasants had to work in all the fields. First they worked in those of the gods, then in those of the emperor, and finally in those that belonged to themselves.

The emperor Topa Inca Yupanqui pays the royal storehouses a visit. He carries his sceptre with him. The official in charge is holding a 'quipu' which records everything kept in the storehouses. If the harvest should fail one year, then everyone in need would be fed from the royal storehouses. In times of plenty, when the storehouses overflowed, the extra food would be given to the people so that they could have a feast.

The land was shared out again every year by an official, and each family was given enough to grow food to live on for that year. Boundaries were well marked; to remove a boundary marker was a terrible crime.

The crops from the gods' fields provided food for the priests and offerings for sacrifice. Crops from the emperor's fields went into the royal storehouses. These supplies provided food for the emperor and his family, nobles and state officials, the army and craftsmen. They were also used to feed people who could not work for themselves, such as the old, the sick, widows and orphans.

The llamas and alpacas which grazed in the highlands were also divided into three groups. The emperor and the gods were given a greater share than the peasants, and no peasant was allowed to have more than ten llamas. The wool of the llamas and alpacas which belonged to the emperor was gathered into the royal storehouses. It was handed out to everybody to make clothes and blankets.

Government records
Although the Incas did not invent a system of writing, they did have a way

16

A woman waters her crop of maize. She has just opened a canal to let water flow into her field. Stone slabs were used to form 'gates' to the irrigation ditches crossing the fields. They were raised to allow water from the main channel to fill the ditches. When enough water had reached the fields, the stones were lowered.

of recording numbers of people and objects with a *quipu* (see page 36). Very strict records were kept to show how many people there were and to which age group they belonged.

Every person in the Inca empire belonged to an *ayllu*. This was a group of families who were all descended from a single ancestor, very much like a clan. A small ayllu had only about 50 members, while a large one had several hundred. The ayllu lived together in a village, or in their own area in a city. Several ayllus in one area together formed a larger group called a *saya*, and two or three sayas formed a province with its own capital city. The provinces were grouped together into the Four Quarters which made up the empire.

Growing up

When a baby was born a local official gave its parents extra land for its support. More land was given for a boy than for a girl. The baby was placed in a cradle with four legs which could either stand on the floor or be strapped to the mother's back. It would stay in the cradle until it was time for it to learn to walk.

When the baby was old enough to be weaned, a special feast was held in its honour and it was given a name. When both boys and girls were about 14 years old there were more ceremonies and feasts, and new names were given to them which they used for the rest of their lives.

Most people had to marry. Every year an important government official visited each district, and all the young unmarried men and women were brought before him. He presented each young man with the bride chosen by him and his family. Any quarrels between young men over who should marry a certain girl would be settled by the official. The weddings were then celebrated with

A herd of alpacas grazing with their young on the 'punas', the high grasslands in the mountains. Alpacas were kept for their long, fine wool. It was regularly shorn and woven into beautiful material.

THE CHOSEN WOMEN

Every now and then a government official visited a village with a special mission. All the girls aged about ten were brought before him and he chose the most beautiful. They were taken to one of the special houses in the large cities. These girls were the *acllacuna*, the Chosen Women. (Young girls who were not chosen were rather unkindly called the *hauasipascuna*, Left-out Girls.) The Chosen Women spent four years being very carefully trained. They were taught weaving and religion and how to run a house. During these four years a few of them would be sacrificed to the gods. This was thought to be a very great honour. The rest of the girls were inspected again once they had finished their schooling. Some, probably the loveliest, were chosen by the emperor to become his wives. He chose others to be given as extra wives to his nobles. The rest became *mamacuna*, Virgins of the Sun (see page 31). They had special religious duties.

LA PRIMERA REINA I.S.
CAPAC POMA GVALLA

A lady from the north of the empire. Men and women were encouraged to wear the clothes of their region. This lady's cloak is fastened with a special pin and she is holding a 'handbag' very much like those of today.

Harvesting the potato crop. The man on the left is using a digging stick, called a 'taclla'. The woman on the right has just loaded a sack of potatoes on her back to carry to the storehouse. The sack is held in place with the help of a special sling which crosses over her forehead. Men and women worked together in the fields of the gods, the emperor and then, finally, in their own.

TRAVAXOS
PAPA ALLAI MITA PA

feasting and dancing. The bridegroom's father would hand over the land given to him by the government at the boy's birth. The government gave the young couple new clothes with which to begin their married life. A house was prepared for them and they paid no taxes for the first year of their marriage.

After the wedding the peasant bridegroom was immediately faced with a busy life working in the fields of the emperor and the gods, as well as in his own. The bride probably had to work even harder, especially when she began to have children. She had to work in the fields as well as cook, clean, look after the children and spin, weave and make clothes for all the family.

Talented boys

Clever and good-looking boys were taken away from their villages to become *yanacona*, special servants of the emperor. Some became pages and servants or worked in the temples, while others held quite important jobs as supervisors. The emperor sometimes gave them to his nobles. It was a great honour to be a yanacona. The boy was close to his master and often won a position of trust and responsibility.

Inca justice

The Incas had a very strict sense of right and wrong and those who broke the rules were severely punished. Crimes such as treason, stealing from the storehouses of the emperor or the gods, or running away with someone else's wife were punishable by death. The offenders would be thrown off a cliff, stoned or clubbed to death. For lesser crimes the criminals were beaten, tortured, blinded, banished or else just publicly told off.

Officials of all levels acted as judges. More serious cases were referred to the higher officials. Punishments varied not only according to the crime, but also according to the reason for the crime. For example, a thief who stole because he was greedy for more than his fair share was given a heavier sentence than the man who stole because he was hungry. If hunger was the cause of the crime, then the official in charge of food supplies in that area would be in trouble for not doing his job properly.

A criminal's age would also be taken into account when his sentence was given. So would any previous convictions. A young offender, who had not been in trouble before, was given a lighter sentence than one who had.

A settled society

Inca society had a place for everyone and work for them to do. Both were settled according to the rank of a child's parents. Only under very special

Tambo Machay near Cuzco. 'Tambos' or rest houses were built by the government for travellers on official business and also for the emperor. At this tambo water still runs into 'baths' through channels. A Peruvian woman sits by the great ruins with a child. She spins wool in much the same way as her Inca ancestors would have done.

circumstances could a person change his or her place in the order of things. Some peasant boys and girls were chosen at an early age to be trained for special duties. They could look forward to a better life. Even those who were unfortunate enough to be sacrificed would live happily in the Next World!

The Incas knew that if they worked and did all that was asked of them, they would be taken care of by the government. They would have a respected place in their village or city. Very few people suffered real hardship under Inca rule. On the other hand, most people did have to work very hard.

A WORKING TAX
People had to work for the state instead of paying taxes. This labour tax was called a *mita*, and the peasants 'paid' it by working on building projects, in the mines, serving in the army, acting as messengers or doing any other necessary task. (Working in the fields of the emperor and the gods did not count as part of this tax.) In this way all the work of the empire was done.

A 12-year-old girl spins wool as she drives her llamas along the road. Her pet dog follows closely behind.

farmers cut steps, or terraces, up the hillsides so that they could grow their crops. While they were building their terraces, the farmers made special ditches so that water could be taken to all the fields when it was needed.

Crops and herds

Maize (also called sweet corn or Indian corn) and potatoes were the most important crops. The farmers also grew many different kinds of vegetables. Gourds and cotton were also grown.

Many farmers had fields at different levels on the mountain slopes, so they could harvest a greater variety of crops. They could grow fruit on the lower, warmer slopes; maize in the middle; and potatoes on the higher, colder slopes.

Llamas and alpacas were grazed on the high grasslands in the mountains. The Incas tamed and kept only three other animals besides llamas and alpacas. Dogs were kept as pets and for hunting, while ducks and guinea pigs were raised for eating.

The farmer's year

Peru lies south of the Equator, so its summer is between December and May. This is the rainy season. Winter, from June to November, is the dry season.

The farmer's year began in August. A great festival was held and *chicha* beer, made from corn, was given to the peasants. Husbands and wives worked

Life on the Land

Most of the people of the Inca empire were farmers, who spent their lives working the fields.

The river valleys on the coast and between the mountains had plenty of water and good soil suitable for farming. Valleys near the coast were fairly level, but the mountain valleys were often narrow with very steep sides. The Inca

A landscape showing mountain terraces built by the Incas. The soil of each terrace was held in place by a stone wall. Special irrigation ditches were built to take water to the terraces. These well-designed systems for growing and watering crops were clearly the work of clever engineers.

> **FOREMEN**
> The Incas appointed foremen from the peasants to be in charge of the work. Some were in charge of as many as 50 people, others were in charge of 10. They were appointed by the *curacas* (see page 13). Apart from the foremen all peasants had the same rank and were supposed to have the same wealth. They were all given land according to the size of their family and everyone was entitled to an equal share from the government storehouses.

side by side, first in the fields belonging to the gods, then in those of the emperor, and finally in their own fields. The first task was to prepare the land. Farmers used manure to make their fields fertile. This included llama dung, human sewage, and on the coast *guano* (bird-droppings).

After they had sown their crops an anxious time began for the farmers. As soon as the first shoots appeared they had to start weeding and watering. The weeding was usually done by women using hoes with bronze blades. Young boys helped to scare away the birds. This went on until December when the rainy season began and *coca* plants were put in. Coca contained an important drug used by doctors as medicine and by the priests.

If the rainy season was late people dressed in mourning and wept. They begged the Thunder god to help them by using his sling to break the jar in which the rains were kept, so that they could pour down on to the thirsty earth. Black llamas and black dogs were tied up and kept hungry and thirsty in the hope that the god would be moved by their sad cries.

The nearer it came to harvest time the more worried the farmers became in case their crops were stolen or destroyed by birds and animals. Some of the men and women were sent to guard the fields armed with slings and rattles to drive

Above left: A gold plate made by the Chimú people. The figure in the centre represents the Earth goddess and the sections round her show when the various crops were planted.

Below: Llamas in an Andean village. They are still used as pack animals today. The Incas rarely killed llamas for food and their wool was only shorn after their death.

away any unwanted intruders. Special huts were built for them if the fields were a long way from the houses.

The harvest was a time of great rejoicing. The early maize was ready in January, but the harvest was not complete until the potatoes were all gathered in June. Potatoes and maize heads were dried to preserve them and then carefully placed in the storehouses of the gods, the emperor and the farmers, according to whose fields they came from.

A modern Peruvian market scene. The crowds and the colour give us a good idea of how Inca markets must have looked. In the background are hanging textiles with geometric patterns, and in the foreground the Peruvians display their fruit and vegetables. Among those the Incas grew were sweet potatoes, tomatoes, peanuts, avocados, chillies, squashes and several kinds of beans.

Food and Clothing

The Incas' food and clothing both depended on the area they lived in, from the hot coastal plain to the cold mountain highlands.

The Incas rarely ate meat, but lived almost entirely on vegetables. They usually had two meals a day, one in the morning and the other in the evening after the day's work was done. One of the most important foods in the warmer areas was maize, which could be boiled, roasted or made into flour and cooked in different ways. It was used to make a kind of flat bread.

In the high country, where maize could not be grown, the Incas made a kind of porridge from plants such as *oca* (an edible root) and *quinoa* (a spinach-like plant whose seeds and leaves were both eaten). Their most usual meal was a soup or stew made of vegetables and flavoured with hot, spicy seasonings. Potatoes were very important. They were usually dried to keep them, but in the high mountains they were sometimes frozen in the snow.

Meat and fish

Llamas were very seldom killed for meat. Guinea pigs provided the only meat that a peasant ate regularly. People who lived within reach of the sea or a lake were able to eat fish.

The royal family and the nobles also ate fresh fish, together with meat, wild duck, and tropical fruits. Food from different parts of the empire was rushed to Cuzco by special relay runners along the royal road.

The favourite drink of the Incas was *chicha*, a beer made from maize. The Incas drank large quantities of it, and at festivals everyone got very drunk.

COOKING FOOD
Food was cooked in clay pots in the open air and sometimes indoors in a clay or stone oven. Wood was very scarce and trees were protected by law. Most people used dried llama dung or the occasional bush as fuel. A fire was started with a firedrill. One stick was held and twirled very quickly against another stick until they began to smoulder. Food was either roasted or boiled and it was served in pottery or wooden dishes, or from gourds.

A soldier from the south of the empire. He is a captain and wears a special hat to show his rank. He carries his cloak over his arm.

Clothes and appearance
We have a very clear idea of the clothes which were worn by the Incas. Some of the pictures in this book are by Poma de Ayala, the grandson of an Inca administrator. He wrote a history of the Incas at the very beginning of the 17th century. He wanted to keep a record of Inca life before it was destroyed. Pottery figures and painted pots show different styles of dress, and clothes worn by the Incas have been found in graves.

Clothes were generally very simple. A man wore a sleeveless, knee-length tunic over a loin cloth. A woman's tunic reached to her ankles. A sash was tied round her waist. Both men and women wore cloaks, which could be fastened across the chest with a pin. Men and women wore head bands, and a woman sometimes wore a veil hanging down the back of her head. Hair styles and head coverings varied from region to region. Sandals were made either of leather or of plaited grass.

Colourful tunics
Near the coast, where it was warm, .clothes were made of cotton. Elsewhere they were made from the wool of llama, alpaca, or the wild vicuna. Some clothes were thick and others were very fine.

Part of a feathered cloak made by the Nazca people who lived in Peru from about AD 200 to 600. The fierce-looking animal is probably a jaguar. Clothes and objects decorated with feathers were popular among many of the ancient peoples of Peru.

Colourful geometric patterns were very popular, and many of the nobles and high-ranking officials wore tunics with a pattern of coloured squares. Inca noblemen also wore gold ear-plugs. The higher a man's rank, the larger his ear-plugs. Some noblemen had very long, pierced ear-lobes that hung almost to the shoulder.

Travelling through the Empire

The Incas built magnificent roads, along which soldiers, supplies, orders and news could travel swiftly and easily.

Two main Inca highways ran from north to south of the empire, one along the coast, the other one through the mountains. Other roads ran across country, connecting the two highways, and lesser roads branched off to every town and village. Each highway was named after the emperor who built it. When the Spaniards arrived about 16,000 kilometres (10,000 miles) of roads had been built, many of them high up in the Andes mountains.

Across country

The roads were long and usually straight and were often paved or cobbled. They ran across the most difficult countryside to the boundaries of the empire. In the deserts the way was marked only with posts. In the mountains the roads zig-zagged up and down very steep slopes, and so steps were cut to make the going easier. Walls on either side of valley roads were often decorated with paintings.

Rivers and marshes were no obstacle, and bridges and causeways were built to carry roads over them. Deep ravines were more difficult to cross. Over them the Incas built special suspension bridges made of ropes of twisted fibres or vines. Three or four thick ropes were bound together and covered with matting and mud to form a platform on which men and llamas could walk. More ropes formed the sides of the bridge and were used as handrails. A Spaniard recorded crossing one of these bridges. It was 60 metres (200 feet) long. The people who lived near these bridges were responsible for keeping them in a good state of repair.

The Incas measured distance by *topos*. A topo was about 7 kilometres (4½ miles) long. On many roads special stones were put up to show the traveller when he had gone a topo.

Roadside buildings

Rest houses called *tambos* were spaced along the roads at a day's travelling distance from one another. They were built by the government for travellers to use on official business. Specially fine tambos were built for the emperor's sole use. The government also built special storehouses near them with enough supplies for an army of 25,000 men.

An Inca road winds its way through the Andes. Trains of llamas carry packs and a relay runner prepares to hand over a quipu. A troop of soldiers marches along and farther up the road a nobleman is carried in his litter. A rope suspension bridge carries the road over a gorge.

Small shelters were placed along each side of the roads at distances of about 1½ kilometres (1 mile) for relay runners. There was enough room in each shelter for two young men, who would be paying their labour tax by being special messengers. A runner was given a package or a message to remember. He set out along the road, running at top speed, to the first relay shelter. There he would pass the package or message to one of the waiting runners who would set off on the next stage of the journey, and so on until the package or message reached its destination.

The Incas had a swift postal service for official use. Packages could pass quickly backwards and forwards across the country. The Spaniards noted with amazement that fresh fish from the sea only took two days to arrive on the emperor's dinner table in Cuzco.

Llama trains

Loads of goods had to be carried either on people's backs or by llamas, the only animals available. The people of the Andes had not invented the wheel so the Incas never had carts or chariots, and indeed they had no animals which could pull them. The horses which had once lived on the American continent had died out thousands of years before the Incas. Llamas were therefore their only means of transport.

Llamas do not travel swiftly. They usually cover only about 15 to 20 kilometres (9 to 12 miles) a day and can carry a load of up to 45 kilograms (100 pounds) in weight. A train of a hundred llamas was driven along the roads by about eight men. Ordinary people had to get permission from the government

ROYAL JOURNEYS
The emperor and the nobles travelled in litters. These were shallow boxes on carrying poles, with room inside for one or two stools for people to sit on. The more splendid ones had canopies or curtains to shield the owner from the sun. One Spanish writer gives a vivid account of the emperor's litter which was made of the best wood and decorated with gold and silver. 'Over the litter there are two high arches of gold set with precious stones, and long mantles fell round all sides of the litter, so as to cover it completely.'

A modern Peruvian leads his train of llamas along an old Inca road beside the ruins of Tambo Machay. In Inca times most llamas were owned by the government. They have long been trained and used to carry loads and are just as important today as they were to the Incas.

A relay runner blowing on a shell to let the next runner know that he is coming.

before they could travel on the roads. Everyone except the nobles had to walk, for llamas cannot carry people on their backs for any distance.

Goods travelled from one end of the empire to the other, and officials of one region exchanged the products of their area with those of another. It was the government that moved goods along the roads and handed them out at certain times to the people. Some private trading was allowed. The emperor Pachacuti is said to have permitted three market days a month when people could exchange goods, or articles they had made in their spare time. As the Incas did not use money, goods were bartered (exchanged for others of a similar value).

Travel by water

The Incas used boats made from bundles of reeds called *totora*, sometimes with sails made of matting. On the northern coast logs of a special light wood called balsa were used to make long rafts. They had masts and sails and some were large enough to carry 50 men and to sail great distances. According to Inca legend, the emperor Topa Inca Yupanqui and his soldiers sailed into the Pacific Ocean, returning with dark-

The guardian of the bridges. It was his duty to make sure that the rope suspension bridges were kept in a good state of repair. Many of them crossed deep ravines with fast-flowing rivers.

A Peruvian woman in a 'totora' reed boat on Lake Titicaca. Her boat is like those made by her Inca ancestors. People living on the coast also made boats and rafts of balsa wood. Fish were caught with traps, nets and hooks and were good food for those who lived near lakes or the sea.

skinned prisoners. One Spanish writer was told that 'much gold and silver, a seat of brass and the hides of animals like horses' were also brought back. They would have used balsa-wood rafts for their expedition.

Topa Inca seems to have been specially good at organizing expeditions using boats and rafts. He is said to have loaded his army into a fleet of canoes and taken them by river into the tropical forests of the Amazon Basin, to punish some Indian tribes who had been causing trouble on his eastern frontier.

SAILING AN INCA RAFT
Thor Heyerdahl, a modern explorer, built a balsa-wood raft to an Inca design. He called his raft *Kon Tiki*. In 1947 he and some friends boarded the *Kon Tiki* and let the wind and the current carry them from Peru across the Pacific Ocean until they landed on one of the Tuamotu Islands. Heyerdahl suggests that a thousand years before the Incas, people were already building similar rafts. Some may have voyaged across the Pacific and landed on Easter Island. This would explain some of the ruins on the island which are very much like those in Peru.

The Builders

The Incas were clever builders. Many of the huge blocks of stone they used for forts and palaces still stand today.

Above left: Inca ruins at Pisac in Peru. Inca buildings were simply shaped and cleverly constructed. Here, rectangular stone blocks have been carefully fitted together and then smoothed down. These ruins show the typical shape of Inca doorways and niches, with the sides sloping inwards towards the top.

The buildings of the Incas varied very much from region to region. The materials they used depended on what was available locally. There was plenty of wood on the hot, damp slopes of the eastern Andes, but in the highlands and on the coast it was very scarce. Stone was the best building material in the cold mountain areas, while *adobe* (mud brick) was used in the warmer, dry coastal regions.

Building skills
The architects and skilled stonemasons who worked on large public buildings were full-time craftsmen, supported by the government. The architects had no paper on which to draw plans. Instead they made models of clay or stone for the workmen to follow. All public building was done by workmen doing their *mita*, the tax which was paid by working for the emperor.

Skilled craftsmen had very few instruments to help them. They probably had plumb-bobs (cords weighted at one end) to make sure that walls were built at the correct angle, and other instruments to check surface levels and measure angles and

These thatched houses in a modern Quechua village in Bolivia are like those built by the Incas. The tiny houses are made of 'adobe' (mud brick). A pile of adobe bricks is stacked in the foreground.

distances. Workmen used only a few simple tools made of wood, stone and bronze, but with these they managed to cut and move huge blocks of stone. Some of these blocks weighed 100 tonnes or more. Each block was roughly cut at the quarry and then taken to the building site. With large numbers of well-organized men using ropes, sledges and earthen ramps, these enormous blocks could be edged into place. They were then cut until they fitted the spaces exactly. Their surfaces were smoothed down but not decorated.

No mortar was used to bind the blocks to one another, but they were fitted together at the site so carefully that even a thin knife blade could not be forced between them. Many Inca buildings which were not deliberately destroyed by the Spaniards are still standing, despite the earthquakes that sometimes send tremors through the country.

Towns and palaces

In towns and villages the most important public buildings and temples were built round a central square. Buildings spread out from the square, usually along quite narrow streets, to the outskirts where the houses of the ordinary people were built. Most buildings in the Inca empire had only one storey, although there were a few buildings of two and three storeys. Water supplies in towns and cities were carefully organized. Covered channels lined with stone carried water from nearby streams to houses in the towns.

Public buildings were of stone but their roofs, like those of private houses, were thatched. Only a very few buildings, which were put up just before the Spaniards came, had stone roofs. The palaces of the emperor were very large, with many rooms grouped around courtyards. In Cuzco a new palace was built for each emperor, and there were many royal palaces built all over the empire in the most important towns.

Above: Peruvian boys among the ruins at Tambo Machay, built by their Inca ancestors. The huge stone blocks are many sided.

FORTRESSES

The Incas were experts at building fortresses made of huge blocks of stone. They were built near all cities as safe places in times of trouble. The picture on the right shows the fort at Sacsahuaman, overlooking Cuzco. It was the greatest Inca fortress. The walls of its three huge terraces were about 18 metres (60 feet) high. A great chain of forts was built along the eastern frontier to keep the empire safe from marauding tribes of Indians. The ruins of some of these forts show how cleverly they were designed to withstand attacks.

Prayers and Sacrifices

Throughout the year the Incas held many religious ceremonies and festivals. Priests offered sacrifices.

Religion played a very important part in the daily life of the Incas. Their chief god was *Viracocha*, the Creator. He was said to have created everything, including the other gods, and he taught men how to live and work. After this he took little interest in the affairs of Earth, so people prayed to him only in times of very great trouble.

The Incas worshipped *Inti*, the Sun, as the most important god after Viracocha and as the father of the royal family. The wife of the Sun was the Moon, the goddess *Mamaquilla*.

Other gods and goddesses also played an important part in daily life. The goddess *Pacamama*, Mother Earth, was probably worshipped most often by the peasants of the highlands, for she would help their crops to grow. *Illapa*, the Thunder god, sent the rain to water the crops. Fishermen on the coast prayed to *Mamacocha*, the Sea goddess.

The emperor leads the ceremonies at one of the great festivals of the Sun god. He is attended by close members of his family, the chief priests and the Virgins of the Sun as he calls on the god to help his people through the coming year. The two great festivals of the Sun were held in December and June. Officials from all over the empire gathered in the great square at Cuzco. At dawn the emperor himself offered chicha beer and a llama was sacrificed.

The Incas thought many objects were sacred. These were known as *huacas*. A huaca could be almost anything, a temple, a hill, or a stone. Each had its own spirit, friendly or unfriendly, which had to be kept in a good humour with offerings, usually of corn or chicha beer.

The priests

The high priest of the Sun, the *vilca-oma*, lived at Cuzco. He was always a brother or uncle of the emperor. He had a council of nine priests from different parts of the empire to help him. The most important priests were all noblemen. Less important priests were often peasant men who were too old to work in the fields. The priests looked after sacred objects, held religious ceremonies, made sacrifices, worked out messages from the gods and cured the sick. They also heard confessions. The Incas thought that people's sins offended the gods, who sent misfortunes as a punishment. It was thought to be a very grave sin not to confess, or to confess only part of a sin. This would anger the gods even more.

The Temple of the Sun

Every large town had its own temple. The greatest temple of the Incas was the *Coricancha* in Cuzco, dedicated to the Sun god. According to Spanish writers its Great Hall of the Sun had only one door, and inside were an altar, images of the gods, sacred objects, and the mummies of past emperors. Many of the objects were of solid gold and it is said that some even decorated the walls.

Virgins of the Sun

Working in the temples were women called *mamacuna*, Virgins of the Sun.

They were specially selected from the Chosen Women (see page 18). They never married, but received three years' extra training to prepare them for a life devoted to the Sun god.

The Virgins of the Sun took part in religious ceremonies and made the chicha beer for them. They also wove the specially fine cloth from which the emperor's clothes were made.

Sacrifices

Sacrifice played an important part in the Inca religion. The usual offerings were of food. Maize and vegetables, birds, guinea pigs, and llamas were sacrificed. Chicha beer was also offered. The drug called *coca* was offered to the gods and was taken by the priests in some ceremonies. It helped them have visions.

Sometimes even human beings were sacrificed. This only happened in times of terrible trouble. It was thought to be a great honour to be chosen, and usually only the most beautiful children and young men and women were sacrificed. They could look forward to a life of comfort in the Next World.

OMENS
The Incas believed that the gods had many ways of getting in touch with them. A rainbow was thought to be a bad omen, and when the emperor Atahuallpa saw a comet shoot across the night sky during his imprisonment by the Spaniards, he immediately gave up all hope of freedom. If the Incas wanted to know what the gods wanted them to do, they sacrificed a llama and examined its internal organs.

Medicine and Death

The Incas had many skilled doctors and surgeons. When they failed, the dead were buried with great care.

The Incas thought most illnesses were sent by the gods as punishments for their sins. Other diseases were thought to be caused by sorcerers. To cause illness was a terrible crime and if a sorcerer was found guilty, he was put to death together with his entire family. Illnesses could also be caused by accidentally meeting an evil spirit carried in the wind or in a stream. Some diseases, like measles and scarlet fever, were unknown before the Spaniards arrived. Large numbers of Incas died because they had no resistance to them. But even before the Spanish conquest there were still many diseases to test the skill of the doctors.

Doctors and medicine

Practising medicine was one of the duties of the priests. There were also some doctors who were ordinary people who had discovered they had a talent for healing. Inca doctors used a variety of treatments. Sometimes they recommended blood letting, purging, dieting or bathing. At other times their treatments included 'good' magic, prayers, fasting, sacrifice, confession of sin and, of course, medicine.

Medicines were usually made from plants. Some were very effective and are still in use. Others had little value as cures. The Incas did not understand the chemical make-up of the things they used, so medicines that cured patients were thought to have magical properties.

One of the Incas' most important medicines was made from the dried leaves of the *coca* plant. Taken in small doses it helps people to overcome hunger and tiredness. In larger doses it

The head of a mummy of the Nazca people. The skull is much longer than normal. The Nazcas, like the later Incas, caused this growth deliberately by binding the heads of their children.

Part of an embroidered textile found with a mummy at Paracas.

LIFE AFTER DEATH

The Incas believed that the spirits of those who had been good during their life on Earth went to join the Sun god. All nobles joined the Sun god whether they had been good or bad! In his kingdom they would enjoy a pleasant life with much feasting and no hard work. Evil people went to a gloomy, underground world where it was always cold and there were only stones to eat.

can be used to kill pain. Inca doctors used it in medicines to cure a number of different illnesses. Tobacco was also used as a medicine. Two modern drugs are made from plants used by the Incas. One of these is cocaine, obtained from *coca*, and the other is quinine, obtained from *cinchona*. The Incas hardly used cinchona at all because malaria, the illness cured by quinine, was unknown before the Spaniards arrived. It was yet another disease that they accidentally introduced into the country.

Surgery

The ancient people of the Andes region were excellent surgeons. Modern surgeons have examined bones found in graves and they have been greatly impressed. One of the most common operations performed, and one of the most skilful, was *trepanning*. Pressure on the brain was relieved by making a hole in the skull. The Incas probably thought this released a demon. Any damaged bone was removed. Injuries to the head must have been common among a war-like people who used clubs and sling stones. The doctors probably gave their patients chicha beer or coca before they carried out their operations, to reduce the pain.

Death

If all remedies failed and the patient died the internal organs were removed and the body completely dried out. It was then wrapped in layers and layers of cloth in a seated position with the chin on the knees. This is known as a mummy. A gold face mask was placed on the mummy of an emperor or a nobleman.

BANISHING ILLNESS

Every September, the Incas held a ceremony in Cuzco, called the *sitowa*. All sick people had to leave the city for a day. The healthy ones had to fast. A special paste made of maize mixed with llama blood was rubbed on their bodies, and some of it was put on their doorsteps. As the Moon appeared that evening, the people gathered in the main square and cried out 'Ills and unhappiness be gone from the country'. Then processions and dances followed, and good health was thought to have triumphed for the next year. In reality disease was not so easy to conquer, in spite of the skill of the doctors. Many people must have suffered and died.

Tombs on a mountainside in Peru. Mummies were placed inside the stone tombs and surrounded by offerings of food, tools and personal ornaments. Care was taken to make sure that each dead person had everything he would need in the Next World.

Part of an ancient human skull from Peru which has been 'trepanned'. An opening was made in it, probably to reduce pressure on the brain. It was later covered up with a silver plate.

Meanwhile the relatives of the dead person put on black clothes and the women cut their hair. A funeral feast was held and a slow dance was performed to sad music. The funeral rites of a dead noble could last for eight days and mourning dress could be worn for a whole year.

The Incas greatly respected their dead ancestors and paid them great honour. Mummies were presented with regular offerings of food and chicha beer. The Incas believed the spirits of the dead liked to have their mummies brought out to join in festivals. All the mummies of past emperors were taken out in a great procession once a year.

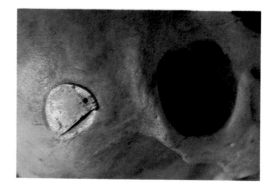

The Craftsmen

The Inca craftsmen were famous for their skill. They were fed and clothed by the government so that as much time as possible could be spent on learning and then practising their crafts.

The people of Peru had been skilled craftsmen long before they came under Inca rule. The Incas valued and encouraged their skills. They knew that people who do highly skilled work need years of training and experience if they are going to do their jobs well. Craftsmen were thought of as government servants, and so everything for their welfare was supplied by the emperor from his storehouses. They were excused from working in the fields and paying their tax to the emperor. Instead, all the things they made belonged to the government and were sent to the emperor's storehouses. A man was expected to teach his craft to his son, who would then follow his father's trade.

Above: A detail of fine Paracas embroidery.
Below: A woman with a back-strap loom.

Weaving

Of all the crafts practised by the people living in the Andes, weaving was the most outstanding. They knew practically every way there is to make cloth, short of using modern machines. We know a great deal about this cloth because many mummies were wrapped in it for burial. The conditions are so dry near the coast that cloth and other articles have been preserved in the graves there, in much the same way as they have been in Egypt.

Left: A back-strap loom being used today.
Below: An Inca pot with painted decorations.

Cloth was made from wool and cotton. Cotton was grown near the coast and was most used there. Llama wool produced a rather coarse thread which was used for things like blankets. The alpaca, a relative of the llama, was kept in large herds especially for its very fine wool. The finest wool came from the vicuna, another relative of the llama. These animals were wild and the Incas hunted them, sheared them, and then let them go. Cotton and wool were kept in storehouses until they were needed, when they were handed out to the people to make their clothes.

Spinning and weaving were done by the women. Wool and cotton were sometimes woven in their natural colours, which ranged from brown to creamy white. They were also dyed in many different shades of colours with dyes from plants and minerals. Some cloth was thick and warm and others were much finer. Some very delicate gauze-like material was so finely woven that it was almost like lace. Many elaborate and colourful patterns were woven into the cloth. Feathers, embroidery, metal sequins and beads were also used to decorate garments. The very best cloth was made by the Chosen Women and the Virgins of the Sun, and was used to make the emperor's clothes. Cloth was woven on back-strap looms like those still used in the area today.

Pottery

The Incas were very skilled potters, although many people today think that Inca pottery was not quite as splendid as that of some of the earlier people living in the Andes region.

The potters mixed their clay with sand or crushed shells, to bind it together. They knew nothing about the wheel so each pot was built up with coils of clay. The pot was smoothed down to remove the bumps made by the clay coils, and then it was decorated. Some pots were moulded in the shape of people or animals. Patterns were usually painted on, but others could be pressed into the clay with a finger-nail or a stick. The pots were then baked.

Metalworking

All mines belonged to the emperor and the metal from them was carefully guarded. Gold and silver were sent straight from the mines to Cuzco, and anyone caught leaving the city with these metals without permission was severely punished.

Skilled craftsmen made objects in gold, platinum and copper, and knew how to mix copper and tin to make bronze. The Incas knew nothing about iron. Most of the things they made were ornaments, such as gold jewellery, models of llamas and face masks for mummies. Only a few tools were made of metal. Many objects were made of gold, silver, and copper hammered into sheets without being heated. Others were made by pouring molten metal into moulds. Furnaces were heated by burning wood, which is scarce and valuable in most of the Andes region. Whenever possible furnaces were built on the slope of a hill. Here there would be a constant draught to fan the fire so that it reached the high temperature needed to melt metal. At other times several men blew on the fire through long tubes.

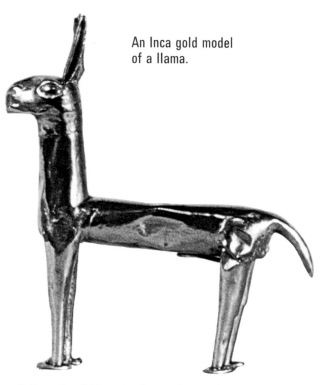

An Inca gold model of a llama.

Below: A gold Inca beaker and part of a silver dish. Very few gold and silver objects from Inca times have survived.

35

Learning and Leisure

Most Incas learned simple skills from their parents. They also learned stories and poems of Inca legend.

As the Inca empire grew, more and more people came under its rule. They spoke perhaps 600 different languages. The language now called Quechua was the language spoken by Incas themselves. It became the official language of the empire, and sons of conquered chiefs had to learn it when they were sent to school in Cuzco. Although Quechua has survived to this day, almost all the other languages are long since forgotten.

'Writing' with knots

The Incas never invented a system of writing, but they did invent a way of recording information. This was done with a *quipu*, a long piece of string on which were tied many other pieces of string of different colours. These had knots tied in them. The colours represented objects, and the tying and placing of the knots showed the

A drawing by Poma de Ayala of a quipu with its 'reader'. Knots were tied in the long pieces of string. In this way complicated records could be kept. Nearby is a frame divided into 20 sections which the Incas used to count with.

different numbers. In this unusual way complicated records of large numbers of goods could be kept. Special quipu readers were trained to understand the records, so that quipus could be sent by messenger from one province of the empire to another. Nobody can 'read' quipus today, so we cannot tell what records they keep.

The Incas' system of counting was in tens, rather like ours. They used special counting frames to help them with their sums. Each frame was divided into 20 sections into which up to 5 pieces of maize were placed.

The Inca calendar was based on the changes in the seasons and on the movements of the stars. The emperor Pachacuti built towers on the hills around Cuzco, and people knew the right time to plant their crops by watching where the Sun rose between them. The year began for the peasants with the planting of their crops, but the official government calendar is said to have begun on 21st December, the day of one of the great festivals dedicated to the Sun.

The Incas also watched the stars. They believed that they could learn

An Aymara Indian from the region of Lake Titicaca playing his pipes. Music and dancing were an important part of Inca festivals. These made a welcome break and everyone drank large quantities of chicha beer. In Cuzco even the mummies of past emperors were carried in procession.

about the future by studying them, and that they received messages from the gods through them. A comet blazing across the night sky meant that some disaster such as war, famine or plague was coming. Eclipses of the Sun were greatly feared as they were thought to signal the coming end of the world.

Learning at school

Most boys and girls did not go to school. Instead they were taught all they needed to know by their parents. But the sons of conquered chiefs and some of the noblemen's sons went to a special school in Cuzco. They stayed there for four years. The boys studied Quechua, the Inca language, in the first year and religion in the second. The third year included studying the quipu and mathematics, and in the fourth year they learned history. The boys also did exercises to strengthen their bodies and keep them fit, and were taught how to use weapons. Laziness and disobedience were punished by caning. The pupils were beaten on the soles of their feet and no one could be given more than ten strokes in any one day.

At the end of the four years, exams were held and prizes were given to the best students. Once a nobleman's son had passed his exams he could have his ears pierced and wear the large gold ear-plugs that marked his noble rank.

Leisure

Most Incas worked very hard indeed, especially the peasant woman whose hands seemed never still. She spun even as she walked along the road with a load on her back. But in spite of all their work the Incas knew how to enjoy themselves. They loved music and dancing and listening to poetry. They also played games.

The Incas played several sports and games and the young noblemen competed publicly in them. There were many less energetic games to play as well. One game was played with objects like dice which were marked with dots representing different numbers. Another game involved pressing seed pods between the fingers to see who could shoot the seeds the farthest.

The Incas were very fond of listening to storytellers and poets. These were special entertainers, popular with everyone including the emperor. They learned poems and stories by heart as well as making up new ones of their own. Love poems were very popular. The emperors were entertained by their own storytellers and poets. When an emperor died a great poem was composed, telling of all his achievements. Unfortunately, the Spaniards did not record many stories or poems and so most of them are now lost forever.

Music and dancing were an important part of Inca life. We can only guess how the music sounded, but we know a good deal about the musical instruments. These included flutes, pipes, whistles, drums, rattles and bells. They were made of wood, reeds, pottery, bone, shell and metal. There were about 150 holidays in the year, including religious ceremonies and festivals of all kinds, when the Incas would play music, dance and, of course, drink chicha beer.

A doll made of reeds and cloth, found in a grave. It was probably thought to have magical properties.

A colourful crowd of modern Quechua Indians at a festival.

The Spanish Conquest

Lured on by rumours of gold, 180 Spaniards gained control of the vast Inca empire.

The days of the Inca empire were about to end. News of the arrival of strange, bearded men in the country came just as the emperor Atahuallpa emerged as the victor over his half-brother Huascar in a civil war which had weakened the empire. Atahuallpa did not take the threat seriously enough until it was too late. The vast Inca empire fell to a small army of Spanish soldiers and adventurers who had come to seek their fortunes in gold.

In 1532 the Spaniard, Francisco Pizarro, landed near the coastal city of Tumbes in the Inca empire, with a force of only 180 men. The Spaniards, who had already conquered Mexico, had heard stories of the gold of South America. Pizarro's expedition was sent to find out if there was any truth in

them. The people of the coast told Pizarro about the great empire, and he made his way towards Cajamarca to meet Atahuallpa. On his way he learned of the recent civil war and of the discontent of some of the recently conquered tribes.

Atahuallpa camped outside Cajamarca with an army of 30,000 men. At first all seemed to go well. The emperor offered the strange newcomers chicha beer and agreed to eat with them the next day. That night Pizarro cunningly hid his men around the square in Cajamarca so that it appeared to be deserted. When Atahuallpa arrived he was met by a Spanish priest reading from a prayer book. The book was handed to Atahuallpa who examined it and then threw it away. He did not understand what it was, nor how holy it was to the Spaniards. This was the opportunity they had been waiting for. As the book touched the ground, Pizarro's hidden army, shouting their battle cry 'Santiago', attacked and Atahuallpa was taken prisoner.

The captive emperor

For eight months the Spaniards held Atahuallpa captive, but they allowed him to rule and to have his wives, servants and courtiers about him. Several of the Spaniards were fascinated

Pizarro who, with only a few men, managed to gain control of the Inca empire. The Spaniards had metal armour, fine metal swords, firearms, small cannon and horses. The Incas' weapons and armour were almost useless against these. For every Spaniard they managed to wound, hundreds of Incas died.

TERROR OF THE INCAS

It is hard for us to understand the awe and terror felt by the Incas when they saw horses, and men riding on horses, for the first time. They may not have realized that man and horse were two separate creatures. One Spaniard fell off his horse. The Incas were horrified to see what they thought was one creature come apart, the two halves able to move about by themselves. Atahuallpa was not afraid. At their first meeting one of the Spaniards galloped his horse straight at him, pulling up only a few inches away from him. Atahuallpa did not even flinch, although some of his men broke ranks and ran. The emperor had them executed.

by this glimpse of Inca life. Others were horrified by it. At last Atahuallpa, realizing how much the Spaniards wanted gold, offered to pay a fabulous ransom to buy his freedom. He would fill his prison cell with gold as high as his hand could reach. He kept his word, to the delight and amazement of the Spaniards, but it did not save him.

As long as Atahuallpa was alive, he was a threat to the Spaniards, who feared that the Incas would attack and free him. They accused him of several crimes and condemned him to be burned to death. To save himself from this fate, so that his body could be properly preserved like those of his ancestors, Atahuallpa agreed to become a Christian. On 29th August 1533 he was baptized and then strangled.

The last Incas
Some of the Inca royal family managed to survive. They may have withdrawn to the mountain stronghold of Machu Picchu. One of them, Titu Cusi, the last great ruler, was highly successful

Atahuallpa meets a Spanish envoy who gallops up on horseback. At the first meeting between the Incas and the Spaniards all seemed to go well.

in resisting the Spaniards. His brother Tupac Amaru, the last ruler, gave himself up to the Spaniards in 1572, only to be executed with his family.

After the death of Tupac Amaru, Machu Picchu was deserted and its buildings gradually crumbled and became overgrown. It was not until 1911 that they were discovered again. Hiram Bingham, an American explorer, had been searching for a lost Inca city by following the account of two Spanish priests who had visited it. Eventually he discovered the ruins of Machu Picchu, perched high on its mountain.

THE LAST PROCESSION
A Spaniard wrote this description of the emperor Titu Cusi, in procession with his court and warriors:

The 399 Indians with their lances, and others from the surrounding country, had made a great theatre for the Inca [the emperor] of red clay. Many lances were drawn up on a hill, and messengers arrived to say that the Inca was coming. The Inca came in front of all, with a headdress of plumes of many colours, a silver plate on his breast, a gold shield in one hand, and a lance all of gold. He wore garters of feathers and fastened to them were small wooden bells. On his head was a diadem and another round his neck. In one hand he had a gilded dagger, and he came in a mask of several colours.

Atahuallpa is strangled by the Spaniards after eight months in captivity.

Some time after the conquest a Spaniard wrote to his king condemning his countrymen's activities in the land of the Incas. 'We have changed the Indians entirely, sowing disorder as we went. This country has gone from one extreme to another. It seems that at one time evil did not exist, today it is good which seems to have disappeared.'

Under Spanish rule

The conquest was a disaster for the Incas, destroying their way of life, their religion and their pride. Spanish priests began at once to convert the new subjects of the king of Spain to the Roman Catholic faith. Those who resisted were harshly punished, often with torture and death. Some people were baptized but many of these, not understanding the meaning of what they had done, still paid homage to their gods. They were also severely punished by the Spanish rulers who had little sympathy for their customs.

Inca lands were divided up and were given out to the Spanish conquerors, the 'Conquistadors', as they were called. The *yanacona*, the special servants of the Incas, were also shared out among the Spaniards. They became no better than slaves. The Conquistadors were often brutal masters. They forced people to work until they died, especially in the mines. They kept them at work by giving them coca, which made their pain and hunger less. The Incas had realized this drug could damage people's health and so had only used it for medicine and for religious purposes, as it gave people visions.

Destroying the heritage

Gold was the Incas' undoing. The Spaniards killed and tortured and worked men to death to get it. Ever since the days of the conquest, grave robbers have been at work destroying valuable evidence in order to tear away the precious metal.

Much of the Incas' knowledge was lost or forgotten. Details of their history, stories of the gods, the way to

The Legacy

The ruins of Machu Picchu, the last stronghold of the Incas, high in the Andes mountains. In the foreground is the Temple of the Sun.

The story of the conquest of the Inca empire is a sad and harsh one. But a conquest, even as harsh as this, rarely manages to destroy a whole people and their way of life.

A modern rope suspension bridge crosses a fast-flowing river. It is made in the same way as those of the Incas.

'read' a quipu and the skill to make the fine cloth all disappeared. Thousands of Incas died from new diseases brought by the Spaniards. Under Inca rule peasants had never been rich, but their needs had been taken care of by the government. After the conquest this system broke down and they became desperately poor.

Inca descendants

However, not quite everything is lost. The descendants of the Incas still live in their mountain homes and they still speak Quechua, the language of the empire. Llamas, now as then, are important to the farmers. Swaying rope bridges like those of the Incas are still made to cross the deep ravines, and the sling and the bola are still in use. Some travellers report that, in remote country districts, a llama is still sacrificed to Mother Earth.

Some of the Spaniards, especially the priests, left accounts of the Inca way of life. School children in Peru are now taught about the greatness of their people's past. Archaeologists are hard at work, digging and recording. Scholars are gradually piecing together details of the remarkable people of the empire of the Incas. *Tahuantinsuyu*, land of the Four Quarters, is well remembered.

As in Inca times, these Peruvian children walk beside a field of corn. Behind them are the thatched roofs of their village.

LOST GOLD?

Magnificent gold works of art were collected and melted down by the Incas to pay their emperor's ransom. One fifth of the ransom was sent to the king of Spain as his share. Legend says that many llama loads of gold were still on their way to Cuzco when news came of Atahuallpa's murder. It is said that this gold was hidden away, and the Spaniards certainly believed this. They tortured many people to reveal the hiding places but none were found. Perhaps some gold has survived and may yet be found in the mountains. It would help to give us a greater idea of the splendour and craftsmanship of the Incas, of which so much was destroyed by the ruthless greed of Pizarro and his men. Only a few gold objects and ornaments have survived to remind us of the beautiful workmanship of the Incas.

Glossary

Pelicans on a rock which is covered in their droppings, known as guano. Sea birds arrive in their hundreds of thousands on the coast of Peru to feed off the shoals of fish brought in by the cold waters of the Humboldt Current. They nest and perch on the rocky islands and the guano is collected by farmers to use as manure on their fields.

Adobe bricks These are made of mud and then dried hard in the sun. They can only be used in dry climates as rain will destroy them.

Alpaca An animal related to the camel and the llama and native to South America. It looks similar to the llama. The Incas kept herds of alpacas for their long fine wool.

Avocado A soft green fruit which grows in tropical areas of America. It is shaped rather like a pear.

Ayllu A related group of families, rather like a clan. Several hundred people could belong to one ayllu.

Balsa The light but strong wood of a tropical American tree. The Incas used it to build rafts.

Blood letting A form of treatment by Inca doctors in which a patient's vein was cut to allow blood to drain from it. This was thought to reduce pressure or fever.

Bola A weapon used in warfare and hunting, made of stones fastened to lengths of string. When it was thrown at an enemy or animal it wrapped itself round the victim's limbs to trip it up and prevent escape.

Chillies Small green or red vegetables. They can be very hot to the taste.

Cinchona A tree or shrub native to South America from which the drug *quinine* is made.

Coca A plant native to America from the dried leaves of which a drug can be obtained. It is the basis of the modern drug called *cocaine.*

Conquistador One of the first Spanish conquerors of America, especially of Mexico and Peru.

Coya The Coya, or queen, was the most important wife of the emperor and was usually his own sister.

Curaca An official under a provincial governor. He could have charge of as many as 10,000 people.

Ear-plugs Gold ornaments, usually circular in shape, worn only by nobles. The larger the ear-plug, the higher the rank. The ears had to be pierced in order to wear them.

Guano Bird droppings which are used as manure. Inca farmers collected it from the coastal areas for their fields.

Incas The members of a few related families from Cuzco who founded the empire. The name is also used of all the people who later came under Inca rule.

Irrigation A system of canals and ditches in which water can be carried to dry areas of land so that crops can grow.

Litter A special 'chair' with carrying poles in which important people travelled.

Llama An animal related to the camel, and native to South America. It was used to carry loads. Its wool produced a rather coarse cloth.

Machu Picchu Now a ruined city high in the Andes mountains. It was the last stronghold of the Incas and was only rediscovered in 1911.

Mita A labour tax which the peasants 'paid' to the state by working on special projects. These included labouring on public buildings, repairing bridges and serving in the army.

Mummies The specially preserved bodies of dead people. The mummies of past emperors

A beautifully decorated pot made by the Nazca people of Peru. Pots like this, with two spouts joined by a tube at the top, are very common in Peru.

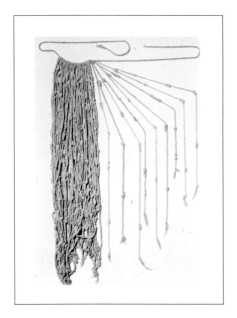

A quipu found preserved in the hot dry sand of the coastal region. Information was recorded by tying knots in the lengths of string. Nobody can 'read' quipus today.

were very carefully looked after and were carried in procession at important religious ceremonies.

Nobles After the emperor, the most important people of the empire. Those of the highest rank were descended from former emperors. Lesser nobles were descended from the chiefs of conquered peoples.

Oca A highland plant, native to Peru, the root of which can be eaten.

Pottery The potters of Peru did not use a wheel to make their pots. Instead, they carefully wound long strips of clay round and round, from the base up. Some pots were moulded in the shape of people or animals and many were beautifully decorated. Pots were made in Peru a long time before the Incas. The Nazca people were highly skilled potters.

Quechua A highland people descended from the Incas. The Quechua language is still spoken today by the Indians of the Andes region.

Quinine A modern drug used to cure malaria. It is obtained from *cinchona,* a tree native to Peru.

Quinoa A highland plant native to Peru. Its seeds are ground and eaten.

Quipu An object made of lengths of coloured string along which knots were tied to record information.

Secondary wives These were less important wives of the emperor. The Coya was the emperor's first wife.

Smallpox An infectious and dangerous disease. It often caused death.

Squash A large fleshy fruit, native to South America.

Terraces Large 'steps' cut into hillsides to increase the area of flat land for farming.

'The' Inca The emperor of the Inca people.

Totora Reeds which the Incas tied into bundles to make boats.

The Incas were able to cultivate steep mountain slopes by terracing them.

Vicuna A wild animal related to the camel and the llama. The Incas hunted it for its very fine wool.

Viracocha The chief god of the Incas. The emperor Viracocha Inca was named after him.

Vicunas grazing in the highlands. These animals were wild and their fine wool was much prized by the Incas. It was used to make the clothes of the nobles.

Index

Bold entries indicate a major mention.
Italic numerals indicate an illustration.

ACKNOWLEDGEMENTS

Photographs : Half title Robert Harding Associates/British Museum ; contents page Tony Morrison (top and centre), ZEFA (bottom) ; page 7 Michael Holford (top), Marion Morrison (bottom) ; 8 Tony Morrison ; 9 Marion Morrison ; 10 Werner Forman Archive/Dallas Museum of Fine Art (top), Michael Holford/British Museum (bottom) ; 11 Tony Morrison (top), Michael Holford/Mujica Gallo, Lima (bottom) ; 12 Tony Morrison ; 13 Tony Morrison (top), Robert Harding Associates/Amano Museum, Lima (bottom) ; 16 Tony Morrison ; 17 Tony Morrison (top), Marion Morrison (bottom) ; 18 Tony Morrison ; 19 Tony Morrison ; 20 Tony Morrison ; 21 Michael Holford/Mujica Gallo, Lima (top left), Tony Morrison (top right), Marion Morrison (bottom) ; 22 Tony Morrison ; 23 Tony Morrison (top), Michael Holford (bottom) ; 26 Robert Harding Associates (top), Tony Morrison (bottom) ; 27 Tony Morrison (top), Marion Morrison (bottom) ; 28 ZEFA (top), Tony Morrison (bottom) ; 29 ZEFA (top), Robert Harding Associates (bottom) ; 32 Tony Morrison (top), ZEFA (bottom) ; 33 ZEFA (top), Tony Morrison (bottom) ; 34 Tony Morrison (top, centre and bottom left), Elizabeth Wiltshire/British Museum (bottom right) ; 35 British Museum (top), Robert Harding Associates/British Museum (bottom) ; 37 Tony Morrison ; 38 Mary Evans Picture Library ; 39 Mary Evans Picture Library ; 40 Spectrum ; 41 ZEFA ; 42 Tony Morrison ; 43 British Museum (top), Marion Morrison (bottom).
Picture research : Ann Horton

AD 1100	SOUTH AMERICA	EUROPE

AD 1100

SOUTH AMERICA

EUROPE

1086 'Domesday Book' (survey of England) completed

1100s The Inca family under Manco Capac settle in Cuzco

1152–1190 Frederick I, Holy Roman Emperor

1241 Mongols withdraw from Europe

1273 Rudolf I, Holy Roman Emperor

1300

1300 Inca Roca takes the title Sapa Inca

1309 Papal See removed to Avignon (until 1377)

1348–1351 Black Death ravages Europe

1370 Expansion of Chimú kingdom on west coast

1400

1420 Brunelleschi begins to build the dome of Florence Cathedral

1431 Jeanne d'Arc burned as a witch in France

1438 Inca empire established in Peru. Pachacuti Inca Yupanqui and his son Topa Inca Yupanqui conquer vast areas

1450 Incas conquer Chimú kingdom

1453 End of Hundred Years' War

1500

1501 Amerigo Vespucci explores the coast of Brazil

1492 Muslims expelled from Granada (Spain)

1517 Reformation begins. Martin Luther nails 'protests' on church door at Wittenberg

1527 Sack of Rome by Holy Roman Emperor

1532 Atahuallpa defeats his brother Huascar in civil war
1533 Francisco Pizarro and his men conquer the Incas and execute Atahuallpa

1572 Defeat and capture of Tupac Amaru, the last Inca ruler

1545 Pope Paul III opens Council of Trent which is to reform the Roman Catholic Church

1580

1580 Spanish conquer Portugal